START-UP HISTORY

SEASIDE HOLIDAYS

Stewart Ross

Evans Brothers Limited

Published by Evans Brothers Limited
2A Portman Mansions
Chiltern Street
London W1U 6NR

© Evans Brothers Limited 2002
Reprinted 2003 (twice), 2005

Produced for Evans Brothers Limited by
White-Thomson Publishing Ltd,
Bridgewater Business Centre,
210 High Street, Lewes, East Sussex BN7 2NH

Printed in China by WKT Company Limited.

Editor: Anna Lee
Consultant: Norah Granger
Designer: Tessa Barwick

Cover (centre): tent-land at Hornsea, Humberside,
  circa 1910.
Cover (top left): on the beach at Margate, 1950s.
Cover (top right): children playing on beach, circa 1940.

British Library Cataloguing in Publication Data

Ross, Stewart
  Seaside holidays. - (Start-up history)
  1.Vacations - History - Juvenile literature
  2.Seaside resorts - History - Juvenile literature
  I.Title
  394.2'69'146

ISBN: 0 237 52409 0

Picture Acknowledgements: Corbis *(cover, top right)* 4, 6,
7, 14, 15 *(top)*, 18, 20; Hulton Getty *(cover, top left)*, 5 *(top)*,
8 *(bottom)*; Andrew Smith/Impact Photos 21; Mary Evans
Picture Library *(cover, centre)*, *(title page)*, 5 *(bottom)*,
10-11, 11, 15 *(bottom)*, 19 *(right)*, 19 *(left)*; Steve
Benbow/The Photolibrary Wales 8 *(top)*; Science and
Society Picture Library 9; Topham Picturepoint 12-13,
16-17.

VISIT OUR WEBSITE
www.evansbooks.co.uk

Contents

Seaside holidays now and in the past

These people are on holiday.
They are at the seaside.

holiday   seaside   years

► **This family is on holiday 50 years ago.**

▼ **Here are people at the seaside almost 100 years ago.**

How are their clothes different from today's clothes?

ago   clothes   different   today

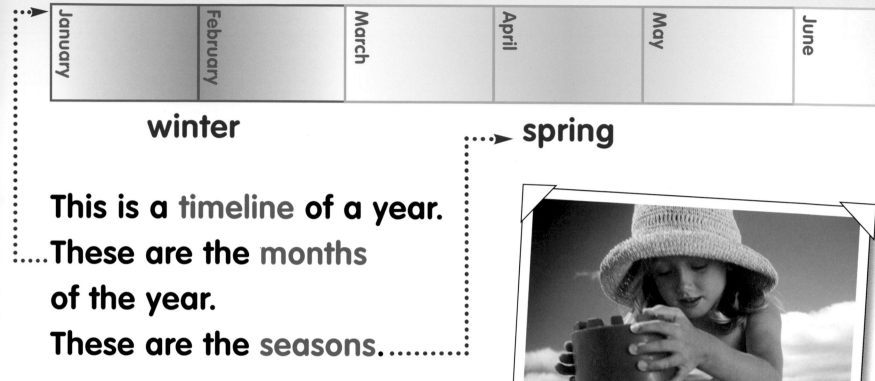

January	February	March	April	May	June

winter

spring

This is a timeline of a year.
These are the months
of the year.
These are the seasons.

We have summer holidays
in July and August.

What other holidays can
you think of?

winter   spring   timeline   months

have holidays?

July | August | September | October | November | December

summer   autumn   winter

Some people like to visit the beach in winter.

seasons   summer   autumn   beach   **7**

How shall we get there?

► These people
are arriving for
a seaside holiday.

They have gone
abroad by **plane**.

◄ This family is going
to the seaside by **car**.

They will stay in
their **caravan**.

abroad plane car

Long ago, steam engines pulled the trains.

The train in this poster is taking people to the seaside.

caravan   steam engines   poster   9

Hooray! We've arrived!

In the past,
people went to the seaside
in buses called charabancs.

How are these charabancs
different from buses today?

past   buses

Can you think of some other ways of going to the seaside?

charabancs

Looking at the past

What a crowded beach!
Is this a modern photograph?
Or was it taken long ago?

You can find out if you look at:

the pram

the food stalls

the men's hats

the women's dresses.

modern   photograph

It is a
photograph of
Herne Bay
in Kent.
It was taken
almost 70 years
ago.

Swimsuits now and then

These pictures are from different times in the past.

The most recent photograph was taken about 5 years ago.

 14

 recent

► **This photograph was taken about 60 years ago.**

◄ **The oldest photograph was taken about 70 years ago.**

How are the swimsuits on these pages different?

Fun at the seaside!

This photograph was taken about 100 years ago.

The people are listening to the band in the bandstand.

Find these things in the picture: houses, clothes, pier, sunshades, bicycles.

Which are the same as nowadays?

Which are different?

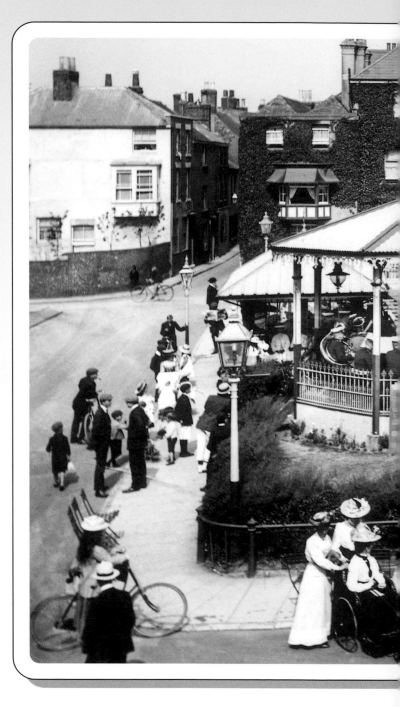

16   band   bandstand   pier

sunshades **nowadays** **17**

More fun at the seaside!

Here is a modern seaside ride.

ride   rollercoaster

► Here is a photograph of a wooden rollercoaster ride from 50 years ago.

▲ The photograph of this family playing cricket was taken about 80 years ago.

What seaside toys are in this picture?

cricket   toys

Punch and Judy

Here are two photographs of children watching
Punch and Judy shows.

One was taken recently. One was taken in the past.

at the beach

What are the differences between them?

How are they the same?

same

Further information for

New history and seaside holiday words listed in the text:

abroad	charabancs	months	Punch and Judy	summer
ago	clothes	nowadays	recent	sunshades
band	cricket	oldest	ride	swimsuits
bandstand	different	past	rollercoaster	timeline
beach	food stalls	photograph	same	today
buses	holiday	pier	seaside	toys
car	long ago	plane	seasons	winter
caravan	modern	poster	steam engine	years

Background Information

A BRIEF CHRONOLOGY

MIDDLE AGES The faithful not expected to work on 'holy days'.

LATE 17th CENTURY ONWARDS 'Grand Tour' of Europe fashionable with the wealthy.
Rising popularity of spas such as Bath and Buxton.

18th CENTURY Seaside resorts become fashionable and popular with the wealthy, e.g. Scarborough, Weymouth and Ramsgate. Bathing machines appear.

EARLY 19th CENTURY First 'tourist' (word first used in 1800) hotels built in romantic beauty spots, e.g. Lake District.
Middle classes visit the seaside.
1840s First seaside excursion trains herald the arrival of working class holidaymakers.
The wealthy flee to more exclusive resorts, or abroad.

MID-19th CENTURY Rise of Blackpool as working class resort. Continental tourism flourishing.
Although only four official public holidays, many northern businesses close for their local wakes or feasts (traditional festivals).

LATE 19th CENTURY

1871 The government introduces four more public holidays. Significant numbers of the working class taking seaside holidays of several nights away from home. Assisted by employers' schemes, Sunday schools and friendly societies.

FIRST HALF OF 20th CENTURY Heyday of the British seaside holiday.
1937 3 million workers have some paid holiday.
First holiday camp (Butlins) opens.
Leisure 'industry' emerging.

Parents and Teachers

1938 Holidays with Pay Act: 14 million workers now have some paid holiday.

1950-2000

1951 25 million people taking holidays in Britain.

1960s Emergence of the mass 'package tour' business.

1971 34 million people taking holidays in Britain. Thereafter the figure declines. 7 million holidaying abroad.

1984 16 million holidaying abroad.
Some once-famous seaside resorts (e.g. Margate) in decline. Others (e.g. Brighton) remain buoyant.

Possible Activities:

Invite an adult to come and talk about their experiences of seaside holidays in the past.

Produce a map of Britain's seaside resorts.

Make a class frieze timeline for the current year and mark all holidays, religious and otherwise, on it.

Make a collection of seaside holiday objects: postcards, buckets and spades, photographs, seaweed, etc.

Some Topics for Discussion:

How have seaside holidays changed from (a) parents' time (b) grandparents' time?

What are the advantages/disadvantages of seaside holidays abroad?

How might holidaymakers be bad for the seaside? (Pollution, environmental damage, etc.)

Further Information

BOOKS

FOR CHILDREN

Holidays by Sallie Purkis (Longman, 1995)

Our Holidays by Stewart Ross (Wayland, 1992)

FOR ADULTS

The Englishman's Holiday: a Social History by J.A.R. Pimlott (Flare Books, 1976)

The English Seaside Resort: a Social History 1750-1914 by J.K. Walton (Leicester University Press, 1983)

The British Seaside: Holidays and Resorts in the Twentieth Century by J.K. Walton (Manchester University Press, 2000)

Sun, Fun & Crowds by Steven Braggs, Diane Harris (Tempus, 2000)

Some Liked it Hot: the British on Holiday at Home and Abroad by Steve Humphries and Miriam Akhtar (Virgin, 2000)

WEBSITES

http://members.netscapeonline.co.uk/sjbraggs/holiday1.htm

http://www.hants.gov.uk/education/ngfl/wardrobe/rboxes/rb3.html

http://www.southwoldpier.demon.co.uk/home.htm

PLACES TO VISIT

Several seaside resorts have fascinating local history museums, for example the Margate Museum, Margate, Kent.

Index